Letts
and
LONSDALE

KS2
Success
SATs

Level 3

Maths

LEARN AND PRACTISE

Paul Broadbent

Contents

Understanding shape

Measuring

Handling data

Glossary

Answers

Word problems

Answering problems

If you have a word problem to solve, try using these four stages.

A bag costs £6.80. What change would there be from a ten-pound note?

1 Read the problem. Try to picture the problem and imagine going through it in real life.
2 Sort out the calculations. Find the **difference** by counting on from £6.80 to £10.
3 Answer the calculations. £10.00 – £6.80 is £3.20.
4 Answer the problem. Look back at the question – what is it asking?

The change from a ten-pound note for the bag is £3.20.

Multi-step problems

Word problems can have different numbers of calculations to answer before you reach the final answer.

One-step problems
There are 185 boys and 217 girls in a school. What is the **total** number of children?

185 + 217 = 402   402 children in total.

Two-step problems
900g of flour and 500g of sugar are mixed together and then divided equally into two bowls. What is the weight of the mixture in each bowl?

Step 1
900g + 500g = 1400g

Step 2
1400 ÷ 2 = 700g

So there is 700g of mixture in each bowl.

Key words   difference   total

Answering problems

1   There are 270g of cake mixture in a bowl. It is divided equally between 9 bun cases. What is the weight of the mixture in each case?   ☐ g

2   Robert is one-fifth of his mother's age. If his mother is 35, how old is Robert?   ☐

3   From Leeds, it is 81km to Manchester and 62km to York. How much further is it from Leeds to Manchester than to York?   ☐ km

4   A hall has 265 chairs in total. At a concert all but 25 chairs are used. How many people are at the concert?   ☐

5   A bike costs £136 and a helmet costs £35. How much do they cost altogether?   £ ☐

6   A regular hexagon has 6 equal sides. Each side is 9cm in length. What is the distance around the whole hexagon?   ☐ cm

6

Multi-step problems

1   There are 4 weeks and 5 days until Rebecca's birthday. How many days is it in total until her birthday?   _____

2   Sam picks 58 apples and Ryan picks 62 apples. They put them together and then divide them equally between 6 bags. How many apples are in each bag?   _____

3   Claire has 43 sweets to put into 9 party bags for her friends. How many will there be in each bag and how many will be left over?   _____

4   Mr Benson posts 3 parcels. Two of the parcels cost £3.20 each and the other parcel costs £2.35. What is the total cost of posting the three parcels?   _____

4

TOTAL MARKS   10

Problem-solving

Reasoning

If you need to think carefully about a way to solve a problem, you are likely to be using reasoning skills to make sense of it. It may help to explain the problem to someone else, describing the way you could try to solve it.

What colour is each shape?

Clues:
- there are three colours used
- yellow is not next to green
- the red square is next to the circle
- the green square is between two red shapes
- the squares are not yellow.

To answer questions like this, draw the shapes and find the clues that give the most help. The third clue shows that the first square is red. That means that the second square is green and the triangle is red. The circle must be yellow.

Always check each clue with your answer to make sure it is correct.

Finding all possibilities

These types of problems often have lots of different choices of answer and the skill is finding the correct one. You need to work systematically, making lists of all the possible answers to find the right one.

Find three **consecutive** numbers that add up to 39.

1 Trial and improvement method:	2 Using reasoning:
14 + 15 + 16 = 45.	39 ÷ 3 = 13.
It must be less:	This must be the middle number:
12 + 13 + 14 = 39.	12 + 13 + 14 = 39.

 Key words   **consecutive**

USING AND APPLYING MATHEMATICS

Reasoning

1 Tom is 9 years old. His father is 36 years old. How many years older is Tom's father? Circle which of these you could use to work this out.

   36 + 9   45 − 9   45 − 34   36 − 9   36 × 9   36 ÷ 9

2 I am thinking of a number. If I double it, the answer is 34. If I subtract 6 from it, the answer is 11. What number am I thinking of?

3 Zoe has some sweets in a box. She takes 5 out and then divides the rest equally into two bags. There are 14 sweets in each bag. How many sweets did she have in the box?

4 Use the clues to work out the colour of each shape.

   Clues:
   - green is between two reds
   - the yellow circle is below a square
   - blue is below green
   - orange is on the right of blue.

   4

Finding all possibilities

1 Three children ate a total of 29 grapes. Each of them ate a different odd number of grapes. If one of them ate 13 grapes, what possible numbers of grapes did the other two eat?

2 Fred bought some burgers and hot-dogs for his friends. Hot-dogs were 50p and burgers were 80p. He spent £6 in total, with 1 more burger than hot-dog bought. How many of each did he buy?

3 Alex spent £2 on 10p and 20p stickers. He bought three times as many 10p stickers as 20p stickers. How many of each sticker did he buy?

   3

Rules and patterns

Number sequences

A **sequence** is a list of numbers written in order.

| 7 8 9 10 11 | | 43 42 41 40 39 |

If you need to find missing numbers in a sequence, look carefully at the numbers you are given. Try to work out the numbers next to these first, then write the others.

127   128   ____   ____   131   ____

So in this sequence, 129 follows 128, then the next number is 130. Which number follows 131?

Number patterns

Counting patterns can have numbers in different steps.
To work out the steps, look at the difference between the numbers.
Look at this counting pattern.

34   37   40   43   ____

Top Tip To help you work out the missing number, draw 'jumps' between each number and write the differences.

This is going up in threes. The next number is 46.

Function machines

You may have questions which ask you to find the numbers going in and coming out of a function machine.

6 → IN ×4 OUT → 24

If you are asked which number goes into the machine, you will need to know the **inverse** or opposite of the function.

The opposite of adding is subtracting.
The opposite of multiplying is dividing.

 Key words   sequence   inverse

Number sequences

Write the missing numbers in each sequence.

1   47   48   ▢   ▢   51   52   ▢

2   163   ▢   165   ▢   167   ▢   169

3   ▢   ▢   79   78   ▢   76   75

4   297   298   299   ▢   ▢   ▢   303

5   402   401   ▢   ▢   398   397   ▢

5

Number patterns

Continue these sequences in both directions.

1   ▢ ▢   51   57   63   ▢ ▢

2   ▢ ▢   32   39   46   ▢ ▢

3   ▢ ▢   40   36   32   ▢ ▢

4   ▢ ▢   81   86   91   ▢ ▢

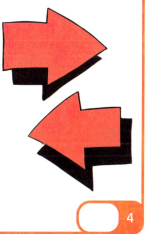

4

Function machines

Write the numbers coming out of these function machines.

1   49   →    IN ÷7 OUT   →   ▢

2   32   →   IN +25 OUT   →   ▢

Write the numbers going into these function machines.

3   ▢   →    IN −9 OUT   →   24

4   ▢   →   IN ×8 OUT   →   56

4

Place value and decimals

4-digit numbers

Look at these numbers and how they are made.

1572   one thousand five hundred and seventy-two

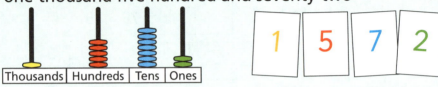

7125   seven thousand one hundred and twenty-five

The position of a **digit** in a number is really important. 1572 and 7125 use the same digits, but they are very different numbers. Always check where you put each digit when you write numbers.

Decimal numbers

Decimal numbers are whole numbers divided into tenths and hundredths. A decimal point is used to separate whole numbers from decimals. Look at these number lines.

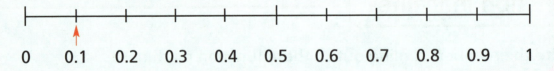

This shows tenths. 0.1 is the same as $\frac{1}{10}$.

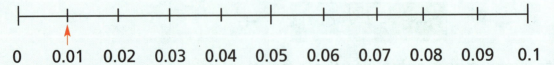

This shows hundredths. 0.01 is the same as $\frac{1}{100}$.

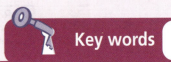

Key words   digit

4-digit numbers

Write these number words as numerals.

1   nine thousand six hundred and forty-two

2   four hundred and twenty-five

3   three thousand two hundred and thirteen

4   one thousand five hundred and ninety-eight

5   six thousand and seventy

6   two thousand and fifty-eight

7   eight thousand three hundred and sixty

8   seven thousand and nine

8

Decimal numbers

Write the missing numbers in the boxes on these number lines.

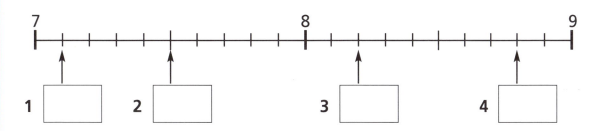

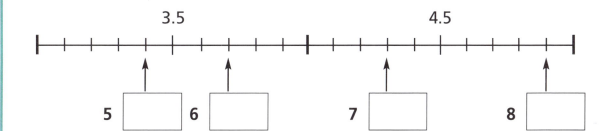

8

TOTAL MARKS   16

Comparing numbers

Comparing numbers

< and > are really useful symbols … but don't get them confused!

< means 'is less than'   45 < 59   45 is less than 59.

> means 'is greater than'   142 > 124   142 is greater than 124.

When you need to compare two numbers, you must look carefully at the value of the digits.

Which is bigger, 87 or 78?

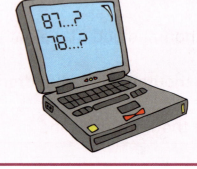

87 is the same as 80 + 7,

78 is the same as 70 + 8,

So 87 is bigger than 78.

Ordering numbers

If you have a list of numbers to put in order, it is a good idea to put the numbers into groups with the same number of digits.

For each group, arrange them in order of size, depending on the place value of the digits.

1 Put these in order, starting with the smallest.

600   3110   305   3200   529   1008   2945

2 Group the hundreds, then the thousands and put them in order.

600   305   529   →   305   529   600

3110   3200   1008   2945   →   1008   2945   3110   3200

3 Put them all together in order.

305   529   600   1008   2945   3110   3200

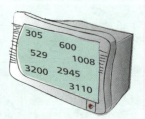

Comparing numbers

Write the correct < or > sign in each box.

1 56 ☐ 93

2 87 ☐ 78

3 44 ☐ 42

4 19 ☐ 61

5 53 ☐ 35

6 220 ☐ 310

7 964 ☐ 938

8 572 ☐ 575

9 414 ☐ 141

10 883 ☐ 838

10

Ordering numbers

Write each set of numbers in order of size, starting with the smallest.

smallest   largest

1 385 198 296 258

☐ ☐ ☐ ☐

2 597 527 592 572

☐ ☐ ☐ ☐

3 1043 4130 3014 4301

☐ ☐ ☐ ☐

4 2665 2556 2656 2566

☐ ☐ ☐ ☐

5 712 294 367 248

☐ ☐ ☐ ☐

6 399 3939 393 9339

☐ ☐ ☐ ☐

6

TOTAL MARKS 16

Estimating

Rounding

Rounding a number to the nearest ten is useful for **estimating**.
A 'round number' is a number ending in zero, such as 10, 20, 30, 40, 50, 60, 70, 80, 90 or 100.

Rounding is easy if you follow these two simple rules.

To round to the nearest 10, look at the 'ones' digit. Then …
1 If it is 5 or more, round up the tens digit.
2 If it is less than 5, the tens digit stays the same.

So 84 rounds down to 80.

137 rounds up to 140.

265 rounds up to 270.

Half-way numbers ending in 5, such as 165, 145 and 385, always round up to the next ten.

Top Tip *Remember, a number is always between two possible 'round' numbers – you just have to choose which one it is nearest to.*

Approximate answers

Estimating is a bit like guessing – but we use information for an **approximate answer**, rather than a wild guess!

Always work out an approximate answer before you calculate, then you will know if your actual answer makes sense. Use rounding skills to work out an approximate answer for the following example.

There are 38 magazines in a box. How many are there in 9 boxes?

38 rounds up to 40.

$40 \times 9 = 360$

38×9 is approximately 360.

 Key words   rounding   estimating   approximate answer

Rounding

Round each of these numbers to the nearest 10.

1 64 → ☐

2 72 → ☐

3 38 → ☐

4 55 → ☐

5 911 → ☐

6 426 → ☐

7 803 → ☐

8 145 → ☐

8

Approximate answers

Circle the number that is nearest to the correct answer for each of these.

1 47 + 32 = 70 80 90

2 19 + 27 = 50 40 30

3 82 + 71 = 140 150 160

4 91 – 18 = 80 70 60

5 66 – 41 = 20 30 40

6 102 – 39 = 80 70 60

7 23 × 7 = 210 200 140

8 38 × 4 = 120 160 180

8

Fractions

Types of fractions

Look at these three types of fraction.

A **proper fraction**, such as $\frac{3}{5}$, which is less than 1.

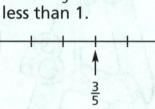

An **improper fraction**, such as $\frac{9}{4}$, which is greater than 1.

$$\frac{9}{4} = 2\frac{1}{4}$$

A **mixed number**, such as $2\frac{1}{4}$, which has whole numbers and fractions.

Parts of a fraction

A fraction has two parts:

$$\frac{2}{3}$$

$2 \leftarrow$ **numerator**

$3 \leftarrow$ **denominator**

Top Tip *The bottom number shows the number of equal parts in total. The top number shows how many equal parts are taken.*

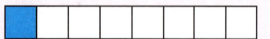

1 part out of 8 is shaded. This shows $\frac{1}{8}$.

7 parts out of 8 are shaded. This shows $\frac{7}{8}$.

Equivalent fractions

Equivalent fractions are worth the same, even though they may look different. Imagine cutting a pizza into quarters and eating two of the pieces. Eating $\frac{2}{4}$ of a pizza is the same as eating $\frac{1}{2}$ of the pizza.

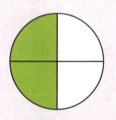

 Key words   **proper fraction**   **improper fraction**   **mixed number**
numerator   **denominator**   **equivalent fractions**

Types of fractions

Put a tick (✔) in each column to complete this table.
One has been done for you.

	$\frac{7}{3}$	$4\frac{2}{5}$	$\frac{10}{9}$	$\frac{4}{5}$	$\frac{3}{7}$	$3\frac{2}{3}$	$\frac{5}{2}$
Proper fraction							
Improper fraction	✔						
Mixed number							

6

Parts of a fraction

Write the fraction of each shape shaded blue.

1 [ ]

2 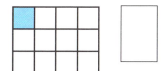 [ ]

3 [ ]

4  [ ]

5  [ ]

6  [ ]

6

Equivalent fractions

Circle two fractions with the same value in each set.

1 $\frac{4}{6}$ $\frac{2}{10}$ $\frac{1}{2}$ $\frac{1}{4}$ $\frac{3}{6}$

2 $\frac{1}{4}$ $\frac{1}{2}$ $\frac{4}{10}$ $\frac{2}{8}$ $\frac{1}{5}$

3 $\frac{2}{6}$ $\frac{1}{4}$ $\frac{1}{2}$ $\frac{1}{3}$ $\frac{1}{5}$

4 $\frac{2}{5}$ $\frac{2}{20}$ $\frac{2}{10}$ $\frac{1}{12}$ $\frac{1}{10}$

5 $\frac{1}{3}$ $\frac{3}{9}$ $\frac{3}{10}$ $\frac{2}{3}$ $\frac{2}{9}$

5

TOTAL MARKS 17

17

Addition and subtraction facts

Number facts

You need to know all of your number bonds to 20.
Number bonds are the addition and subtraction facts within 20.

Here are some examples.

7 + 7	7 + 8	7 + 9
16 – 6	16 – 5	16 – 4

You can use these facts to add and subtract tens.

3 + 5 = 8   9 – 6 = 3

3 tens + 5 tens = 8 tens   9 tens – 6 tens = 3 tens

30 + 50 = 80   90 – 60 = 30

 Top Tip *If you start at 0 and count on in tens, you will find multiples of 10.*
10 20 30 40 50 60 70 80 90 100

Trios

The three numbers 8, 5 and 3 are called a trio.
They can make four addition and subtraction facts.

3 + 5 = 8   5 + 3 = 8   8 – 5 = 3   8 – 3 = 5

If you learn your addition facts, you can use them to help with subtraction.

4 + 9 = 13   ☐ – 9 = 4   13 – ☐ = 9

 Top Tip *Remember that 4 + 6 gives the same answer as 6 + 4. It doesn't matter which way round you add. Once you know one fact, you know the other.*

Key words   multiple

Number facts

Answer these additions and subtractions.

1 2 + 9 = ☐   **6** 70 – 50 = ☐

2 12 – 4 = ☐   **7** 30 + 40 = ☐

3 8 + 7 = ☐   **8** 90 – 80 = ☐

4 16 – 3 = ☐   **9** 60 + 20 = ☐

5 11 + 6 = ☐   **10** 100 – 50 = ☐

10

Trios

Use these trios to find the missing numbers in each addition and subtraction.

4   5   9   3   10   7   8   6   14

1 4 + 5 = ☐   **2** 9 – ☐ = 5   **3** 7 + 3 = ☐

4 ☐ – 7 = 3   **5** 14 – 8 = ☐   **6** 8 + ☐ = 14

6

TOTAL MARKS 16

Multiplication facts

Times tables

Learning your tables will make the rest of the maths easier. Once you know these, you will never forget them.

On the grid, try to find $6 \times 4 = 24$.

You will see it is written twice, showing that the answer is the same for both: $6 \times 4 = 4 \times 6$.

×	1	2	3	4	5	6	7	8	9	10
1	1	2	3	4	5	6	7	8	9	10
2	2	4	6	8	10	12	14	16	18	20
3	3	6	9	12	15	18	21	24	27	30
4	4	8	12	16	20	24	28	32	36	40
5	5	10	15	20	25	30	35	40	45	50
6	6	12	18	24	30	36	42	48	54	60
10	10	20	30	40	50	60	70	80	90	100

Write down any facts you are not sure of and try to learn them. Use other facts to help.

8×3 is **double** 4×3.

9×3 is 3 less than 10×3, which is 27.

7×4 is double 7×2. Double 14 is 28.

Once you learn these, you can try your 7, 8 and 9 times tables.

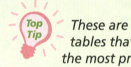

Top Tip These are the facts for the tables that probably cause the most problems:

6 x 3   7 x 3   8 x 3   9 x 3
6 x 4   7 x 4   8 x 4   9 x 4

Learn one fact a day – it will only take 8 days!

Multiples

It is useful to be able to recognise multiples of 2, 5 and 10.

Multiples of 2 end in **0, 2, 4, 6, 8**.

18 is a multiple of 2.

Multiples of 5 end in **0** or **5**.

35 is a multiple of 5.

Multiples of 10 end in **0**.

60 is a multiple of 2, 5 and 10.

 Key words   double   even number

Times tables

Answer these questions.

1 $7 \times 2 =$ ☐

2 $5 \times 4 =$ ☐

3 $3 \times 6 =$ ☐

4 $4 \times 4 =$ ☐

5 $9 \times 5 =$ ☐

6 What is three multiplied by nine? ☐

7 Multiply seven by four. ☐

8 Double eight. ☐

9 There are six cakes in a packet. How many cakes are there in five packets? ☐

10 There are seven days in a week. How many days are there in ten weeks? ☐

Top Tip *Remember that even numbers are all multiples of 2.*

10

Multiples

Use this list of multiples to answer each question.

| 50 | 15 | 8 | 14 | 9 | 20 |

1 Which numbers are multiples of 10? _____

2 Which numbers are multiples of 2? _____

3 Which numbers are multiples of 5? _____

4 Which number is a multiple of 5, but not a multiple of 2 or 10? _____

5 Which two numbers are multiples of 2, but not multiples of 10 or 5? _____

6 Which two numbers are multiples of 3? _____

6

TOTAL MARKS 16

Division facts

Dividing

Dividing is the opposite of multiplying. It is the same as sharing or grouping.

These both show 15 divided by 3.

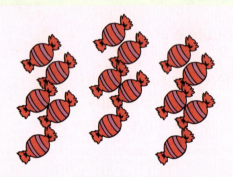 

15 sweets shared between 3.
There are 5 in each group.

$15 ÷ 3 = 5$

15 sweets grouped into 3s.
There are 5 groups.

$15 ÷ 3 = 5$

Top Tip *Remember that multiplication and division are inverses (opposites). Because of this, division can be checked by multiplying.*
$35 ÷ 5 = $ ➡ $5 x 7 = 35$ ➡ so $35 ÷ 5 = 7$

Missing number problems

15, 5 and 3 are a special set of numbers. We call them a trio, as you will have read on page 18.

$3 × 5 = 15$ $5 × 3 = 15$ $15 ÷ 3 = 5$ $15 ÷ 5 = 3$

Knowing your trios can help work out missing number problems.
2, 6 and 12 are another trio. Use them to find the missing numbers.

$2 × \_\_\_\_ = 12$ $\_\_\_\_ × 2 = 12$ $12 ÷ \_\_\_\_ = 6$ $\_\_\_\_ ÷ 6 = 2$

 Key words   inverse

Dividing

1 Divide twelve by three. ☐

2 How many fives are there in forty? ☐

3 What is twenty-eight shared equally between four? ☐

4 What is half of eighteen? ☐

5 A class of 32 children are put into 4 equal teams. How many children are in each team? ☐

6 How many 5p stamps can be bought with 30p? ☐

7 27 counters are divided equally between 3 pots. How many counters will there be in each pot? ☐

8 There are 28g of yoghurt in a pot. Half the yoghurt has been eaten. How much yoghurt is left? ☐ g

8

Missing number problems

Write the missing numbers.

1 $70 \div \boxed{} = 10$

2 $\boxed{} \times 2 = 16$

3 $4 \times \boxed{} = 20$

4 $45 \div \boxed{} = 5$

5 $\boxed{} \times 3 = 18$

6 $\boxed{} \div 2 = 7$

7 $5 \times \boxed{} = 25$

8 $24 \div \boxed{} = 4$

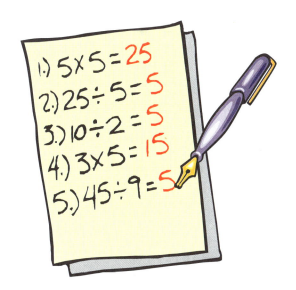

1.) $5 \times 5 = 25$
2.) $25 \div 5 = 5$
3.) $10 \div 2 = 5$
4.) $3 \times 5 = 15$
5.) $45 \div 9 = 5$

8

Mental addition and subtraction

Adding 2-digit numbers

If you need to add two big numbers, it helps to break the numbers up and add the tens, then add the ones.

15 + 37 = _____

Use these three steps.

1 Hold the bigger number in your head: 37.

2 Break 15 into 10 + 5. Then add the tens: 37 + 10 = 47.

3 Finally, add the ones: 47 + 5 = 52.

Counting on

A really good method for a take-away or subtraction is to find the difference between the numbers by counting on.

What is the difference between 18 and 34?

18   20   34

This number line shows exactly what goes on in your head.

Count on from 18 to 20. Hold the 2 in your head.

20 to 34 is 14.   14 + 2 is 16.   So 34 – 18 = 16.

2

Top Tip *If it helps, draw a quick number line and show the steps. Remember to put the smallest number on the left and the largest on the right.*

Adding 2-digit numbers

Calculate these additions and write the matching letters to find the code words. Each letter is worth one mark.

1   14 + 23 = ☐ ➜ ☐

     64 + 11 = ☐ ➜ ☐

     34 + 24 = ☐ ➜ ☐

2   28 + 35 = ☐ ➜ ☐

     59 + 22 = ☐ ➜ ☐

     33 + 16 = ☐ ➜ ☐

3   24 + 25 = ☐ ➜ ☐

     37 + 44 = ☐ ➜ ☐

     48 + 27 = ☐ ➜ ☐

     19 + 39 = ☐ ➜ ☐

4   23 + 35 = ☐ ➜ ☐

     45 + 36 = ☐ ➜ ☐

     56 + 19 = ☐ ➜ ☐

     17 + 46 = ☐ ➜ ☐

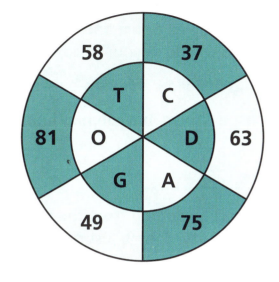

14

Counting on

Read and answer these questions.

1   What is the difference between 29 and 52?

2   How much less is 38 than 83?

3   Calculate the difference between 47 and 15.

4   How much more is 64 than 43?

5   Find the difference between 16 and 39.

6   What is the difference between 21 and 78?

6

Written addition

Written method for adding

If you are given a sum and the numbers are too big or there are too many numbers to add in your head, then you need to use a written method.

417 + 265 Follow this step-by-step method.

1 Write them in a **column**, lining up the units digits.

```
  417
+ 265
```

2 Start by adding from the right-hand column, the units column. Any total over 9, just put the tens digit under the next column.

```
  417
+ 265
    2
  1
```

3 Now do the same with the tens column. Keep going left until all the columns have been added.

```
  417
+ 265
  682
  1
```

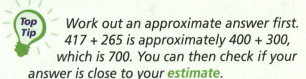
Top Tip *Work out an approximate answer first. 417 + 265 is approximately 400 + 300, which is 700. You can then check if your answer is close to your estimate.*

Adding money

It can be a bit confusing if you need to add mixed amounts of pounds and pence. What is the total cost of a drink that is £1.60 and a cake at 79p?

Try changing the pence to pounds, lining up the decimal point.

```
  1.60
+ 0.79
  2.39
  1
```

£1.60   79p

The total cost is £2.39.

 Key words   column   estimate

Written method for adding

Calculate these additions.

1   408
     + 257
     _____

2   361
     + 429
     _____

3   515
     + 185
     _____

4   146
     + 277
     _____

5 Add together 362 and 539.

6 What is the total of
      444 and 198?

7 Calculate 207 + 595.

8 Add 487 and 416.

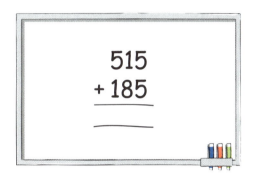

515
+185
_____

8

Adding money

Calculate the total cost.

£3.40   £1.59   88p
£1.09   75p

1   £ [   ]   **5**   £ [   ]

2   £ [   ]   **6**  £ [   ]

3    £ [   ]   **7**   £ [   ]

4   £ [   ]   **8**    £ [   ]

8

TOTAL MARKS 16

Written subtraction

Column method

If you cannot work out a subtraction in your head, this is one method you can try.

What is 874 subtract 138?

Step 1	Step 2	Step 3
Rename 70 + 4 as 60 + 14.	60 − 30 = 30	800 − 100 = 700
14 − 8 = 6		

$$8\,^6 7\,^1 4$$
$$-\ 1\ 3\ 8$$
$$6$$

$$8\,^6 7\,^1 4$$
$$-\ 1\ 3\ 8$$
$$3\ 6$$

$$8\,^6 7\,^1 4$$
$$-\ 1\ 3\ 8$$
$$7\ 3\ 6$$

Top Tip — *Important! Remember to always take the bottom number away from the top number.*

Number line method

Another written method is to use a number line to find the difference between the numbers by counting on.

What is 173 subtract 138?

1   Draw a blank number line from 138 to 173.

2   Count on to 140, then to 173 to find the difference.

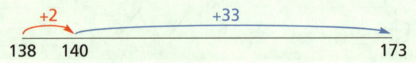

+2   +33

138   140   173

3   Add up all the jumps.

2 + 33 = 35, so the difference between 138 and 173 is 35.

Column method

Complete these subtractions.

1
```
    4 9 3
  – 1 5 5
  ───────
```

2
```
    7 0 2
  – 6 8 2
  ───────
```

3
```
    5 3 7
  – 1 4 9
  ───────
```

4
```
    8 2 6
  – 2 1 8
  ───────
```

5 Subtract 165 from 368.

6 What number is 294 less than 750?

7 Calculate 411 – 172.

8 What is 603 minus 359?

9 What is 527 subtract 188?

9

Number line method

Use the number lines to answer these.

1 What is the difference between 436 and 481?

436   481

2 What is the difference between 597 and 617?

597   617

3 What is the difference between 215 and 400?

215   400

4 What is the difference between 350 and 523?

350   523

4

TOTAL MARKS 13

Multiplication

Mental calculations

If you know your tables, then multiplying numbers to 20 by a single digit can be worked out in your head.

What is 13 multiplied by 4?

Use these three steps.

1 Multiply the tens: 10 × 4 = 40.

2 Multiply the units: 3 × 4 = 12.

3 Add the two parts: 40 + 12 = 52.

Top Tip *To multiply tens by a single digit, work out the fact and then make it ten times bigger:*

60 x 4 = 6 x 4 x 10 = 24 x 10 = 240

Written methods

To work out a multiplication such as 38 × 5, you need to be able to multiply multiples of 10.

38 = 30 + 8

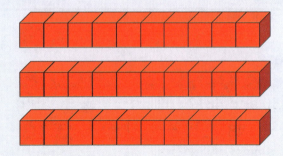   +

38 × 5   →   30 × 5 = 150

8 × 5   =   40 +

38 × 5 = 190

Look at these two methods for this.

```
    3 8
  ×   5
  ───────
    190
      4
```

x	30	8
5	150	40

150 + 40 = 190

Answers

PAGE 5

Answering problems
1	30g	**4**	240
2	7 years old	**5**	£171
3	19km	**6**	54cm

Multi-step problems
1 33
2 20
3 4 sweets in a bag and 7 left over
4 £8.75

PAGE 7

Reasoning
1 27 years older
   36 – 9
2 17
3 33
4

Red   Green   Red

Yellow   Blue   Orange

Finding all possibilities
1 1 and 15, 3 and 13, 5 and 11, 7 and 9
2 4 hot-dogs and 5 burgers
3 4 20p stickers and 12 10p stickers

PAGE 9

Number sequences
1 47, 48, **49**, **50**, 51, 52, **53**
2 163, **164**, 165, **166**, 167, **168**, 169
3 **81**, **80**, 79, 78, **77**, 76, 75
4 297, 298, 299, **300**, **301**, **302**, 303
5 402, 401, **400**, **399**, 398, 397, **396**

Number patterns
1 **39**, **45**, 51, 57, 63, **69**, **75**
2 **18**, **25**, 32, 39, 46, **53**, **60**
3 **48**, **44**, 40, 36, 32, **28**, **24**
4 **71**, **76**, 81, 86, 91, **96**, **101**

Function machines
1	7	**3**	33
2	57	**4**	7

PAGE 11

4-digit numbers
1	9642	**5**	6070
2	425	**6**	2058
3	3213	**7**	8360
4	1598	**8**	7009

Decimal numbers
1	7.1	**5**	3.4
2	7.5	**6**	3.7
3	8.2	**7**	4.3
4	8.8	**8**	4.9

PAGE 13

Comparing numbers
1	56 < 93	**6**	220 < 310
2	87 > 78	**7**	964 > 938
3	44 > 42	**8**	572 < 575
4	19 < 61	**9**	414 > 141
5	53 > 35	**10**	883 > 838

Ordering numbers
1 198, 258, 296, 385
2 527, 572, 592, 597
3 1043, 3014, 4130, 4301
4 2556, 2566, 2656, 2665
5 248, 294, 367, 712
6 393, 399, 3939, 9339

PAGE 15

Rounding
1	60	**5**	910
2	70	**6**	430
3	40	**7**	800
4	60	**8**	150

Approximate answers
1	80	**5**	30
2	50	**6**	60
3	150	**7**	140
4	70	**8**	160

PAGE 17

Types of fractions

	$\frac{7}{3}$	$4\frac{2}{5}$	$\frac{10}{9}$	$\frac{4}{5}$	$\frac{3}{7}$	$3\frac{2}{3}$	$\frac{5}{2}$
Proper fraction				✔	✔		
Improper fraction	✔		✔				✔
Mixed number		✔				✔	

Parts of a fraction
1	$\frac{1}{5}$	**4**	$\frac{4}{7}$
2	$\frac{1}{12}$	**5**	$\frac{3}{10}$
3	$\frac{5}{6}$	**6**	$\frac{7}{9}$

Equivalent fractions
1	$\frac{1}{2}$ and $\frac{3}{6}$	**4**	$\frac{2}{20}$ and $\frac{1}{10}$
2	$\frac{1}{4}$ and $\frac{2}{8}$	**5**	$\frac{1}{3}$ and $\frac{3}{9}$
3	$\frac{2}{6}$ and $\frac{1}{3}$		

PAGE 19
Number facts
1	11	6	20
2	8	7	70
3	15	8	10
4	13	9	80
5	17	10	50

Trios
1	9	4	10
2	4	5	6
3	10	6	6

PAGE 21
Times tables
1	14	6	27
2	20	7	28
3	18	8	16
4	16	9	30
5	45	10	70

Multiples
1	50 and 20	4	15
2	50, 8, 14 and 20	5	8 and 14
3	50, 15 and 20	6	15 and 9

PAGE 23
Dividing
1	4	5	8
2	8	6	6
3	7	7	9
4	9	8	14g

Missing number problems
1	7	5	6
2	8	6	14
3	5	7	5
4	9	8	6

PAGE 25
Adding 2-digit numbers
1 37 → c
   75 → a
   58 → t
2 63 → d
   81 → o
   49 → g

3 49 → g
   81 → o
   75 → a
   58 → t
4 58 → t
   81 → o
   75 → a
   63 → d

Counting on
1	23	4	21
2	45	5	23
3	32	6	57

PAGE 27
Written method for adding
1	665	3	700
2	790	4	423
5	901	7	802
6	642	8	903

Adding money
1	£4.99	5	£2.34
2	£2.18	6	£1.76
3	£4.15	7	£4.49
4	£1.97	8	£2.72

PAGE 29
Column method
1	338	6	456
2	20	7	239
3	388	8	244
4	608	9	339
5	203		

Number line method
1	45	3	185
2	20	4	173

PAGE 31
Mental calculations
×	14	19	17
5	70	95	85
3	42	57	51

Written methods
1 112
2 324
3

120	27

120 + 27 = 147

4

350	15

350 + 15 = 365

5	74	8	220
6	285	9	252
7	172	10	171

PAGE 33
Doubling and halving
1	18	5	43
2	32	6	13
3	74	7	29
4	90	8	24

Division and remainders
1	22r2	5	47
2	19r3	6	4
3	22r3	7	4
4	17r1		

PAGE 35
Fractions of shapes
1	$\frac{1}{2}$	4	$\frac{1}{4}$
2	$\frac{1}{3}$	5	$\frac{1}{4}$
3	$\frac{1}{5}$	6	$\frac{1}{2}$

Fractions and division

1	4	6	12
2	4	7	4
3	7	8	8
4	2	9	3
5	6		

PAGE 37

Lines of symmetry

1

2

3

4 Any one of these lines of symmetry

5

6 Either of these lines of symmetry

7

8 Any one of these lines of symmetry

Reflections

1

2

3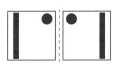

4

PAGE 39

Polygons

1 6 sides – hexagon
2 6 sides – hexagon
3 3 sides – triangle
4 5 sides – pentagon
5 8 sides – octagon
6 7 sides – heptagon

Regular polygons

Shape	Property of shape		
	4 sides	A regular shape	1 or more right angles
▭	✔	✗	✔
⬡	✗	✔	✗
⬠	✗	✗	✔
◼	✔	✔	✔
△	✗	✔	✗

PAGE 41

Names of 3D shapes

1 cylinder
2 sphere
3 cube
4 cylinder
5 triangular prism
6 cuboid
7 cone
8 cuboid

Parts of solid shapes

1 4
2 cube
3 tetrahedron
4 sphere

PAGE 43

Right angles

1

2

3

4

5

6

7

8

Types of angles

1 c
2 b
3 a
4 e
5 a
6 c and d
7 b
8 b

PAGE 45

Coordinates

1 (1,2) 2 (2,4) 3 (4,8)

4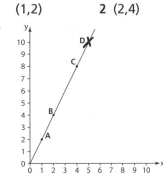

Points of the compass

1 & 2

Directions

1 South
2 West
3 South-East

PAGE 47

Units of measure
1 14cm
2 2 litre
3 2m
4 60g
5 3km

Converting units
1 4000ml
2 5500m
3 700cm
4 3500g
5 120mm

Reading scales
1 2cm
2 25mm

PAGE 49

Finding perimeters
1 124m
2 5m
3 11cm
4 7cm

Finding areas
1 4 square cm
2 7 square cm
3 9 square cm
4 6 square cm

PAGE 51

Time facts
1 28 days
2 90 minutes
3 Monday
4 36 months
5 1 day
6 30th April

Telling the time

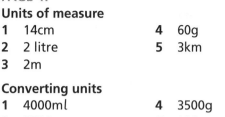

PAGE 53

Bar charts
1 90 km/h
2 Hare
3

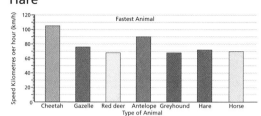

4 Antelope

Pictograms
1 Tuesday
2 4
3 Thursday
4 11
5 3

PAGE 55

Venn diagrams

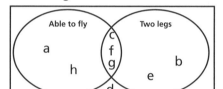

Carroll diagrams

	1 or more right angles	No right angles
Quadrilateral	c, d	f, h
Not a quadrilateral	b, e	a, g

Letts Educational
4 Grosvenor Place, London SW1X 7DL
School enquiries: 015395 64911/65921
Parent & student enquiries: 015395 64913
E-mail: mail@lettsandlonsdale.co.uk

Website: www.letts-educational.com

First published 2008

Editorial and design: 2ibooks [publishing solutions] Cambridge

Author: Paul Broadbent
Book concept and development: Helen Jacobs, Publishing Director
Editorial: Sophie London, Senior Commissioning Editor
        Katy Knight, Editorial Assistant
Illustrators: Andy Roberts and Phillip Burrows
Cover design: Angela English

British Library Cataloging in Publication Data. A CIP record of this book is available from the British Library.

ISBN 9781843158806

Text, design and illustration © Letts Educational Limited 2008

Printed in Italy

Mental calculations

Write the missing numbers to complete this multiplication grid.

×	14	19	17
5			
3			

6

Written methods

Answer these.

1 28 × 4 =

$$\begin{array}{r} 28 \\ \times\ \ 4 \\ \hline \end{array}$$

2 54 × 6 =

$$\begin{array}{r} 54 \\ \times\ \ 6 \\ \hline \end{array}$$

3 49 × 3 =

4 73 × 5 =

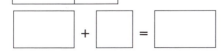

5 What is thirty-seven multiplied by two?

6 Calculate 95 × 3.

7 A shop has 86 pairs of shoes. How many shoes are there altogether?

8 Golf balls are sold in packs of five. How many balls will there be in 44 packs?

9 A baker has baked enough rolls to fill 63 bags with 4 rolls each. How many bread rolls did he bake in total?

10 A school uses three 57-seater buses for a trip to a museum. All the seats are filled. How many tickets will be needed for the museum?

10

TOTAL MARKS 16

Division

Doubling and halving

An important thing to remember about division is that it is the inverse or opposite of multiplication.

$$40 \div 2 = \underline{\hspace{1cm}} \qquad 20 \times 2 = 40$$

It is very useful to be able to double and **halve** numbers. Look at this doubling machine.

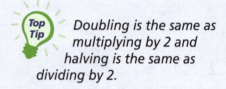

> When a number goes in, it is doubled.
> If 32 goes in, 64 comes out.

What if you put numbers backwards through the machine? Can you see that it becomes a halving machine?

> For example, half of 28 is 14 and half of 64 is 32.

Top Tip *Doubling is the same as multiplying by 2 and halving is the same as dividing by 2.*

Halving is the opposite of doubling.

Division and remainders

Many division answers are not exact. They have an amount left over. For example, if you wanted to put 35 pencils into boxes, with 4 pencils in each box, there would be some pencils left over. If a number cannot be divided exactly, it leaves a **remainder**.

Work out how many groups of 4 are in 35 and what is left over:

```
      8 r 3
  4 | 3 5
  –   3 2   (4 × 8)     35 ÷ 4 = 8 remainder 3
  ─────────
      3
```

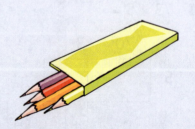

 Key words halve   remainder

LEARN

CALCULATING

Doubling and halving

Write the missing numbers for each function machine.

1 9

2 16

3 37

4 45

5 86

6 26

7 58

8 48

8

Division and remainders

Answer these questions. Use the box to show your method for the first four.

1 $3 \overline{| 68}$ =

2 $79 \div 4$ =

3 $4 \overline{| 91}$ =

4 $52 \div 3$ =

5 Circle the number that has a remainder of 2 when divided by 5.

33   68   47   54

6 What is the remainder when you divide fifty-two by six?

7 Twenty-five eggs are put into boxes holding six eggs each.
There is one egg left over.
How many egg boxes are used?

7

Fractions of quantities

Fractions of shapes

When you are asked to work out fractions of shapes, you may need to work out equivalent fractions. Remember to find the number of equal parts (the denominator or bottom number of the fraction) and then how many parts are shaded (the numerator or top number of the fraction).

What fraction of the rectangle is shaded?

The rectangle is divided into 8 equal parts and 2 parts are shaded.

$$\frac{2}{8} \quad \frac{\div 2}{\div 2} = \frac{1}{4}$$

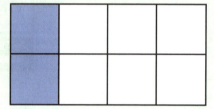

Fractions and division

Look at these examples.

What is:

| $\frac{1}{3}$ of 15? | $\frac{1}{5}$ of 20? | $\frac{1}{4}$ of 12? |

 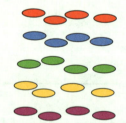 

These all have 1 as a numerator, so simply divide by the denominator.

$\frac{1}{3}$ of 15	$\frac{1}{5}$ of 20	$\frac{1}{4}$ of 12
is	is	is
$15 \div 3 = 5$	$20 \div 5 = 4$	$12 \div 4 = 3$

Fractions of shapes

What fraction of each shape is shaded red?

1

4

2

5

3

6

Fractions and division

Use the balloons to answer these questions.

1   What is $\frac{1}{3}$ of 12?

2   What is $\frac{1}{4}$ of 16?

3   What is $\frac{1}{2}$ of 14?

4   What is $\frac{1}{5}$ of 10?

There are 24 balloons of different shapes and colours in a pack.
How many of each type of balloon are there?

5 $\frac{1}{4}$ are red   red balloons

6 $\frac{1}{2}$ are yellow   yellow balloons

7 $\frac{1}{6}$ are blue   blue balloons

8 $\frac{1}{3}$ are large balloons   large balloons

9 $\frac{1}{8}$ are long balloons   long balloons

Symmetry

Lines of symmetry

Some shapes are **symmetrical** – they have lines of symmetry. Look at the shape.

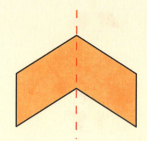

If you imagine it folded down the middle, the two sides would look exactly the same. That fold line is the line of symmetry and shows if a shape or pattern is symmetrical.

These letters are symmetrical.
Can you see the lines of symmetry?

Reflections

You may be asked to draw the reflection of a picture or pattern so that it is symmetrical. The mirror line is always drawn to help and the shapes are usually drawn on a grid. Use the squares on the grid to help you work out the position of each corner of the shape.

Draw the reflection of this shape.

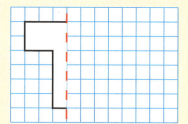

Imagine the line is a mirror. Draw dots on each corner and count the squares across, so that each point is reflected.

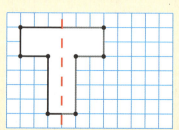

When a mirror is put on the line of symmetry, the half shape and its reflection show the whole shape. Practise using a small mirror to help you find symmetrical shapes.

Key words | **symmetrical**

Lines of symmetry

Draw one line of symmetry on each of these shapes.

1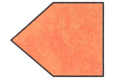

2

3

4

5

6

7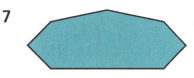

8

8

Reflections

Complete these reflections.

1 Use a ruler to draw lines to make a symmetrical shape about the mirror line.

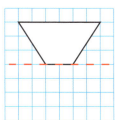

2 Shade in the reflection of this shape. You may use a mirror.

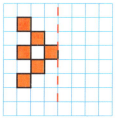

3 Here is a square with a design on it. The square is reflected in the mirror line. Draw the missing stripe and circle on the reflected square.

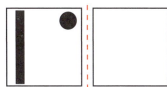

4 Draw the reflection of this triangle.

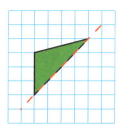

4

TOTAL MARKS   12

2D shapes

Polygons

Any shape with straight sides is called a **polygon**.
The name of the polygon tells you the number of sides.

3 sides	Triangle	
4 sides	Quadrilateral	
5 sides	Pentagon	
6 sides	Hexagon	
7 sides	Heptagon	
8 sides	Octagon	

Regular polygons

Regular polygons are shapes with all sides of equal length and all angles the same size.

Some regular shapes have special names.

A regular triangle is an **equilateral triangle**.

A regular quadrilateral is a **square**.

Another special four-sided shape is a **rectangle**. It has four **right angles** and two pairs of **parallel** sides, which are the same length.

 When you look at shapes, check their sides and angles. Remember that parallel sides never meet and right angles are like square angles.

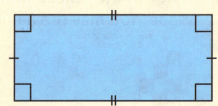

 Key words   **polygon   right angle   parallel**

Polygons

Count the number of sides and write the name of each shape.

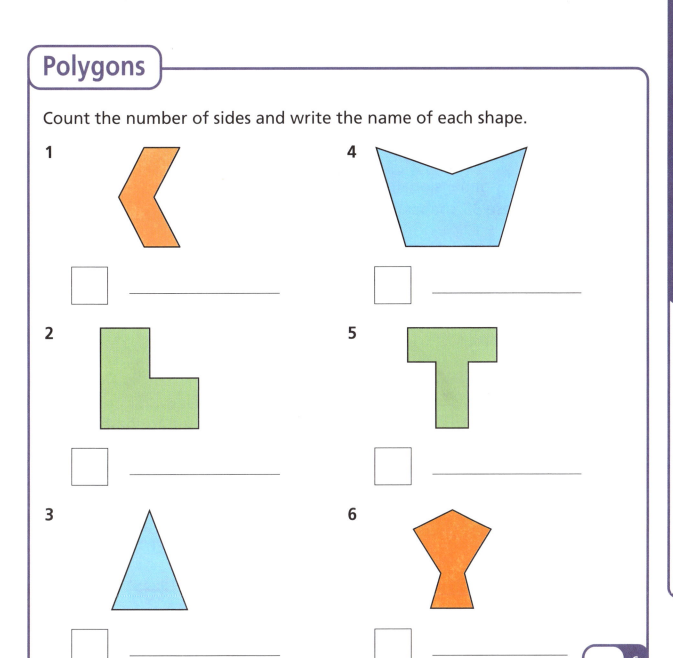

1 ☐ _____

2 ☐ _____

3 ☐ _____

4 ☐ _____

5 ☐ _____

6 ☐ _____

6

Regular polygons

Complete this table. Write in the missing cross (✗) or tick (✔) in each space.

Shape	Property of shape		
	4 sides	A regular shape	1 or more right angles
(yellow rectangle)		✗	
(blue hexagon)	✗		
(green pentagon)			✔
(orange square)	✔		
(red triangle)			✗

10

TOTAL MARKS 16

3D solids

Names of 3D shapes

Solid shapes are 3-dimensional. You need to learn the names and properties of these 3D shapes.

cube

cuboid

cylinder

tetrahedron

cone

triangular prism

sphere

square-based pyramid

 Top Tip *A cube is a special cuboid and a cuboid is a type of prism. Can you see how a cuboid has some properties similar to a triangular prism?*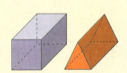

Parts of solid shapes

Solid shapes are made up of **faces**, **edges** and **vertices** or corners.

A face is a surface of a solid.

An edge is where two faces meet.

A vertex is where three or more edges meet.

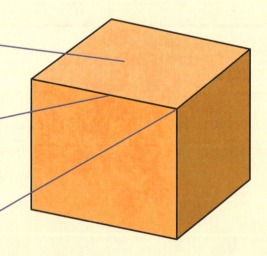

 Top Tip *Some shapes have flat faces and some are curved. A cylinder has 2 flat faces and 1 curved face.*

 Key words   **face**   **edge**   **vertex/vertices**

LEARN

UNDERSTANDING SHAPE

Names of 3D shapes

Write the shape name of each of these everyday objects.

1

_____

2

_____

3

_____

4

_____

5

_____

6

_____

7

_____

8

_____

8

Parts of solid shapes

Read and answer these questions.

1 How many faces are triangles on a square-based pyramid? _____

2 Which solid shape has 6 square faces and 12 edges? _____

3 I am thinking of a 3D shape. It has 4 triangle
   faces and 4 vertices. What shape am I thinking of? _____

4 Which 3D shape has one curved face and no edges? _____

4

TOTAL MARKS 12

Angles

Right angles

Corners of doors, windows, books and tables all show right angles.

These are **square angles** and can be seen all around us.

A right angle is a quarter turn, **clockwise** or **anticlockwise**.

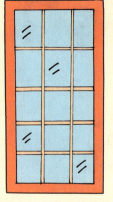

Squares and rectangles have four right angles – one at each corner.

Types of angles

An angle is a measure of turn between two lines. Angles are measured in degrees (°).

There are 360° in a full circle.

90°	90°
90°	90°

These are special angles to remember.

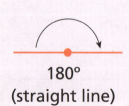 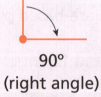 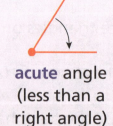 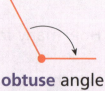

| 180° (straight line) | 90° (right angle) | **acute** angle (less than a right angle) | **obtuse** angle (between 90° and 180°) |

 Use a right-angle corner from a piece of paper to compare angles, to see if they are acute or obtuse.

Key words   clockwise   anticlockwise   acute   obtuse

Right angles

Circle all of the right angles on each shape.

1   2   3   4

Read the instructions and circle the arrow pointing in the correct direction.

5   This arrow is rotated 90° clockwise.

6   This arrow is rotated 90° anticlockwise.

7   This arrow is rotated 90° anticlockwise.

8   This arrow is rotated 90° clockwise.

8

Types of angles

Look at these angles and answer the questions.

a   b   c   d e

1 Which is the smallest angle? ☐   6 Which two angles are acute?

2 Which angle is a straight line? ☐   ☐ and ☐

3 Which is a right angle? ☐   7 Which angle is 180°? ☐

4 Which angle is obtuse? ☐   8 Which is the largest angle? ☐

5 Which angle is 90°? ☐

8

PRACTISE

UNDERSTANDING SHAPE

TOTAL MARKS 16

43

Position and direction

Coordinates

Coordinates are used to show the exact position of a point on a grid.

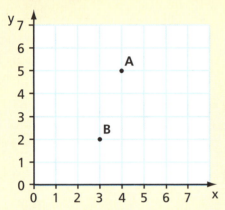

The coordinates of **A** are (4,5).

The coordinates of **B** are (3,2).

Coordinates are always written in brackets and separated by a comma.

Remember to read the **horizontal** number along the bottom and then the **vertical** number up the side.

Points of the compass

It is useful to know the points of the compass. North and South are opposite each other, as are East and West. In between these are the other four points. Look at the way their names always start with North or South.

 To remember the order of the four main directions, look at the initials NESW. A well-known saying to learn this order is Naughty Elephants Squirt Water!

Directions

Clockwise and anticlockwise are instructions for moving in different directions. Quarter turns, half turns and whole turns are used to describe how far to turn.

This arrow has moved a quarter turn clockwise.

This arrow has moved a half turn anticlockwise.

A whole turn is a complete circle. This is a whole turn clockwise.

Key words   horizontal   vertical

Coordinates

1 Circle the correct coordinates for point **A**.

(1,1)   (1,2)   (2,1)   (2,2)

2 Write the coordinates for point **B**.

(☐ , ☐)

3 Write the coordinates for point **C**.

(☐ , ☐)

4 Draw a cross at (5,10) and label it **D**.

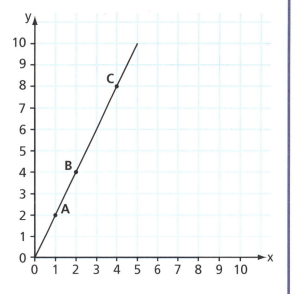

☐ 4

Points of the compass

The arrow labelled N is pointing North.

1 Label the arrows pointing South, West and East.

2 Colour the arrow pointing North-West.

☐ 2

Directions

Look at the compass points to help you answer these.

1 If I face North and make a half turn clockwise, which direction will I be facing? _____

2 If I face South and make a quarter turn clockwise, which direction will I be facing? _____

3 If I face North-West and make a half turn anticlockwise, which direction will I be facing? _____

☐ 3

TOTAL MARKS ☐ 9

Measures

Units of measure

Length, weight (or mass) and capacity are all measured using different units. Try to learn these:

Length	1 centimetre (cm) = 10 millimetres (mm)
	1 metre (m) = 100 centimetres (cm)
	1 kilometre (km) = 1000 metres (m)
Weight	1 kilogram (kg) = 1000 grams (g)
Capacity	1 litre (*l*) = 1000 millilitres (ml)

Top Tip *Remember to always write the units in your answers. There is a big difference between 100g and 100kg!*

Converting units

Once you know these **equivalent** measures, then you can convert from one unit to another. This always means multiplying or dividing by 10, 100 or 1000, depending on what you are converting.

My finger is 6.3cm or 63mm long.

A lemonade bottle holds 3000ml or 3 litres.

This cake weighs 1.3kg or 1300g.

20 times around a 400m running track is 8000m or 8km.

Reading scales

A scale is the marking of lines to help us measure, e.g. up the side of a jug, on weighing scales or on a ruler. You need to read them carefully, using these steps:

1 Look at the unit – is it ml, cm, mm, g … ?

2 If the line is level with a number, read off that number.

3 If the line is between numbers, work out what each mark means and count on or back.

Key words **equivalent**

Units of measure

Underline the amount each item is most likely to measure.

1 My pencil is (14mm) (14cm) (14m) (14km) long.

2 I bought a (2ml) (20ml) (2 litre) (20 litre) carton of milk.

3 The classroom door is (2mm) (2cm) (2m) (2km) high.

4 An apple weighs (6g) (60g) (6kg) (60kg).

5 I travel (3mm) (3cm) (3m) (3km) to school every day.

5

Converting units

Answer these questions.

1 How many millilitres are there in four litres? ____ ml

2 How many metres are there in five and a half kilometres? ____ m

3 How many centimetres are there in seven metres? ____ cm

4 How many grams are there in three and a half kilograms? ____ g

5 How many millimetres are there in twelve centimetres? ____ mm

5

Reading scales

Measure these sides with a ruler.

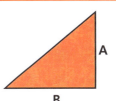

1 Use a ruler to measure the length of side **A**.
   Give your answer in centimetres. ____ cm

2 Measure accurately the length of side **B**.
   Give your answer in millimetres. ____ mm

2

TOTAL MARKS ____ **12**

Perimeter and area

Finding perimeters

The **perimeter** of a shape is simply the distance all the way around the edge. These two shapes have the same perimeter of 16cm.

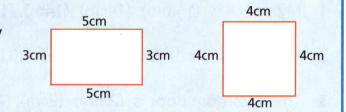

If the shape has straight sides, add up the lengths of all the sides. These may be given, or you may need to measure carefully along each of the sides using a ruler.

3cm + 3cm + 4cm + 4cm + 6cm = 20cm

The perimeter of this shape is 20cm.

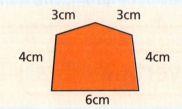

If the shape has curved sides, a piece of string or cotton may be useful. Go around the edge of the shape and then measure the length of the piece of thread.

This shape has a perimeter of 10cm.

Finding areas

The **area** of a shape is the amount of surface that it covers. You can often measure the area of shapes by counting squares.

These shapes both have an area of 8 squares.

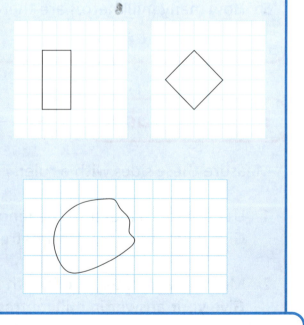

If the shape is not made up from whole squares, count all the squares that are bigger than a half.

This shape has an area of approximately 12 squares.

 Key words   perimeter   area

Finding perimeters

Answer these questions.

1 This playground measures 35m by 27m.
What is the perimeter of this playground?

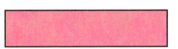

35m

27m

 m

2 A square carpet has a perimeter of 20m.
How long is one of its sides?

 m

3 Measure the sides of this rectangle.
What is the perimeter of this rectangle?

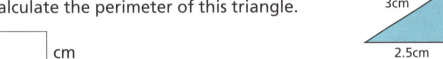 cm

4 Calculate the perimeter of this triangle.

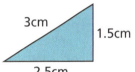

3cm   1.5cm

2.5cm

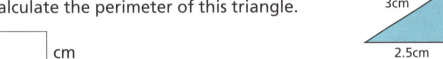 cm

4

Finding areas

Count the squares and write the areas for each shape.

1cm

1cm

1

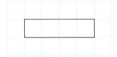

_____ square cm

3

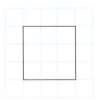

_____ square cm

2

_____ square cm

4

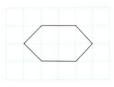

_____ square cm

4

TOTAL MARKS   8

Reading the time

Time facts

These are some time facts to learn. Cover each one up and see how many you can remember.

1 minute	= 60 seconds	1 week	= 7 days	
1 hour	= 60 minutes	1 fortnight	= 14 days	
1 day	= 24 hours	1 year	= 12 months	= 365 days
		leap year	= 366 days	

Use the 'knuckle method' to learn the days of the months:

31 days: January, March, May, July, August, October, December.

All the 'knuckle months' have 31 days. February has 28 days (29 days in a **leap year**) and April, June, September and November have 30 days.

Or you can remember:
30 days has September, April, June and November.
All the rest have 31, except February which has 28 days clear and 29 each leap year.

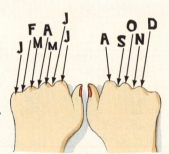

Telling the time

Reading a circular clock face.

If you find it difficult to tell the time, then follow these three easy steps.

1. Look at the short hour hand on your clock or watch and say the last hour that this has gone past. This has gone past the 5, so it is past 5 o'clock.

2. Look at the longer minute hand and count around in fives from the top to the hand: 5, 10, 15, 20, 25, 30, 35, 40.

3. Say aloud the hour followed by the number of minutes – so you say 5.40, which means 40 minutes past 5.

 Key words leap year

LEARN

MEASURING

50

Time facts

Answer these questions.

1 How many days are there in four weeks? _____

2 A film is an hour and a half long.
How many minutes is this? _____

3 If today is Monday 10th August, what day
of the week will 17th August be? _____

4 How many months are there in three years? _____

5 How many more days are there in a leap year
than a normal year? _____

6 If today is 1st May, what was the date yesterday? _____

6

Telling the time

Draw the missing hands to show these times. Remember to draw the hour
hand shorter than the minute hand.

1

quarter past ten

2

6.10

3

twenty past eight

4

11.25

5

quarter to one

6

9.55

6

TOTAL MARKS 12

Handling data

Bar charts

Bar charts are a useful way of showing information. To understand bar charts and other types of graph, look carefully at the different parts of the graph.

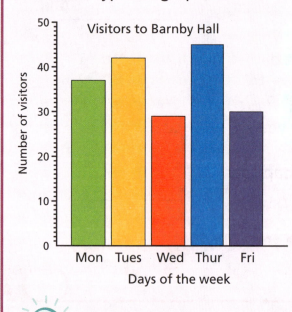

Visitors to Barnby Hall

1 Read the title – what is it all about? Is there any other information given?

2 Look at the **axis** labels – these should explain the lines that go up and across.

3 Work out the scale – look carefully at the numbers. Do they go up in 1s, 2s, 5s, 10s … ?

4 Compare the bars – read them across to work out the amounts.

Top Tip *The scale is very important. This graph goes up in tens and some of the bars are between tens. For example, there were between 40 and 50 visitors on Tuesday. To read this, go across from the top of the bar and count on from 40 to 42.*

Pictograms

Pictograms use symbols or pictures, where each symbol represents a certain number of items.

This is a record of the numbers of frogs seen crossing a road in a morning.

Time	Number of frogs
7:00 – 8:00	🐸 🐸 🐸 🐸
8:00 – 9:00	🐸 🐸 🐸 🐸 🐸 🐸
9:00 – 10:00	🐸 🐸 🐸 🐸 🐸 🐸 🐸 🐸 🐸 🐸
10:00 – 11:00	🐸 🐸 🐸 🐸 🐸 🐸 🐸
11:00 – 12:00	🐸 🐸 🐸

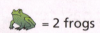 = 2 frogs

Top Tip *Check what each individual picture stands for. This shows that 12 frogs were seen between 8.00 and 9.00am.*

 Key words   axis

Bar charts

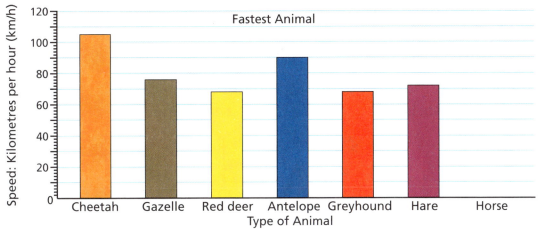

1 What speed can an antelope run? _____ km/h

2 Which is fastest, a greyhound or a hare? _____

3 The fastest speed recorded for a horse is 70km/h. Draw a bar to show this on the chart.

4 Which animal runs 20km/h faster than the horse? _____

4

Pictograms

This pictogram shows the number of eggs collected from a group of chickens each day.

Days of the week	Number of eggs
Monday	◯ ◯
Tuesday	◯ ◯ ◯ ◜
Wednesday	◯ ◯ ◯
Thursday	◯ ◜
Friday	◯ ◯
Saturday	◯ ◯ ◜
Sunday	◯

1 On which day were the most eggs collected?

_____

2 How many eggs were collected on Friday? _____

3 On which day were three eggs collected? _____

4 How many eggs were collected in total on Monday and Tuesday? _____

5 How many more eggs were collected on Saturday than Sunday? _____

5

TOTAL MARKS 9

Sorting diagrams

Venn diagrams

To sort these shapes into groups, you could use a **Venn diagram**.
This Venn diagram sorts the shapes by colour and shape.

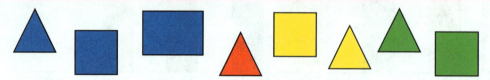

This shows the set of triangles.

This shows the set of blue shapes.

This shows shapes that are not blue or triangles.

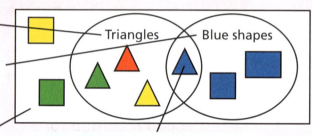

Triangles   Blue shapes

This shows blue shapes that are triangles.

Carroll diagrams

Carroll diagrams are very similar to Venn diagrams, but they use a grid rather than circles.

You can use a Carroll diagram to sort shapes, objects or numbers.

16   34   13   27   43   39   22   19   40   45

This shows even numbers that are greater than 20.

	even numbers	not even numbers
greater than 20	22, 34, 40	27, 39, 43, 45
not greater than 20	16	13, 19

This shows numbers that are not even and are greater than 20.

This shows the set of even numbers not greater than 20.

This shows the set of numbers not greater than 20 and not even.

 Key words   Venn diagram   Carroll diagram

LEARN

HANDLING DATA

Venn diagrams

Write the letter for each creature in the correct section of this Venn diagram. Then you could have a go at drawing them too!

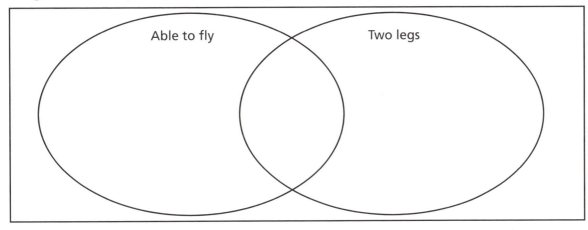

Able to fly   Two legs

a bee

b human

c seagull

d spider

e penguin

f owl

g bat

h butterfly

8

Carroll diagrams

Use these shapes to complete this Carroll diagram. You can either write the shape's letter or draw in the shape.

a   b   c   d   e   f   g   h

	1 or more right angles	No right angles
Quadrilateral		
Not a quadrilateral		

8

TOTAL MARKS 16

Glossary

acute an angle smaller than a right angle

anticlockwise turning in this direction

approximate answer a 'rough' answer – near to the real answer

area the area of a shape is the amount of surface that it covers

axis (plural is axes) the horizontal and vertical lines on a graph

Carroll diagram a grid used to sort things into groups or sets

clockwise turning in this direction

column a vertical arrangement of numbers, words or objects going up or down

consecutive one after the other in order. For example, 15, 16 and 17 are consecutive numbers

denominator the bottom number of a fraction, the number of parts it is divided into. Example: $\frac{2}{3}$

difference the difference between two numbers is the amount that one number is greater than the other. The difference between 18 and 21 is 3

digit there are 10 digits: 0 1 2 3 4 5 6 7 8 and 9 that make all the numbers we use

double make something twice as big, or multiply by 2

edge where two faces of a solid shape meet

equivalent two numbers or measures are equivalent if they are the same or equal

equivalent fractions these are equal fractions. Example: $\frac{1}{2} = \frac{2}{4} = \frac{3}{6}$

estimate is like a good guess

even number a number that can be divided exactly by 2. Even numbers end in 0 2 4 6 or 8

face the flat side of a solid shape

halve to cut an object or a group of objects into two equal parts, so there is $\frac{1}{2}$ in each

horizontal a horizontal line is a straight level line across, in the same direction as the horizon

improper fraction any fraction which is greater than 1, such as $\frac{5}{3}$, $\frac{8}{5}$ or $\frac{6}{2}$

inverse the opposite or reverse – addition is the inverse of subtraction

leap year every four years there are 366 days in a year. The extra day is the 29th February

mixed number any whole number and fraction written together, such as $2\frac{1}{2}$, $4\frac{3}{5}$ or $1\frac{3}{10}$

multiple a multiple is a number made by multiplying together two other numbers

numerator the top number of a fraction. Example: $\frac{3}{5}$

obtuse an angle less than 180° (a straight line) but greater than 90° (a right angle)

parallel lines that are parallel never meet and the distance between the lines remains the same

perimeter the distance all the way around the edge of a shape or object

polygon any straight-sided flat shape

proper fraction any fraction which is less than 1, such as $\frac{2}{3}$, $\frac{3}{5}$ or $\frac{1}{10}$

remainder if a number cannot be divided exactly by another number, there is a whole number answer with an amount left over, called a remainder

right angle a quarter turn. The corner of a square is a right angle

rounding changing a number to the nearest ten. A 'round number' is a number ending in zero: 10, 20, 30, 40, 50, 60, 70, 80, 90 or 100

sequence a list of numbers which usually have a pattern. They are often numbers written in order

symmetrical when two halves of a shape or pattern are identical

total when you add some numbers, the answer is the total

Venn diagram a diagram that shows groups of things by putting circles around them

vertical a line that is straight up or down, at right angles to a horizontal line

vertices (single is vertex) the corners of 3D shapes, where edges meet